Impact 360

INSTITUTE

your college launch story:

six things every parent must do

JOHN D. BASIE, Ph.D.

Impact 360
INSTITUTE

Published in Pine Mountain, Georgia,
by Impact 360 Institute
(www.impact360institute.org).
Know. Be. Live.

Impact 360 Institute titles may be purchased in bulk
for educational, business, fundraising, or sales promotional use.
For information, please email info@impact360institute.org.

Editorial team: John Basie, Jonathan Morrow, Miriam Drennan
Cover design: Ellen Parker Bibb

Softcover ISBN: 978-0-9915977-6-5
e-Book ISBN: 978-0-9915977-7-2

Printed in the United States of America

Impact 360

INSTITUTE

We exist to impact culture by creating Christ-centered worldview and leadership opportunities.

Impact 360 Institute was born when John and Trudy Cathy White recognized an increasing need for equipping young adults in the area of godly leadership. Impact 360 Institute appreciates the value of holistic learning and holds to a three-pillar philosophy of know, be, live: know why you believe, be who God created you to be, live what you learn.

Impact 360
PROPEL

Propel Student Leadership Conference is a 4-day catalytic leadership conference for high school students where they will learn what it means to be Christ-centered and how to influence their peers.

Impact 360
IMMERSION

Immersion is a two-week transformational worldview and leadership experience for high school students in which they will learn what they be believe, why they believe it, and how to live it out in the real world.

Impact 360
GAP YEAR

Impact 360 Gap Year is a nine-month Christian worldview and leadership experience located in Pine Mountain, Georgia serving students 18-20 years old. The mission is to equip members of future generations to become Christ-centered servant leaders.

Impact 360
SCHOLARS

Know, Be, and Live – type equipping during all four years of a college student's education to prepare them for maximum leadership influence in their various God-given callings.

Impact 360
MASTERS

The mission of Impact 360 Masters is to equip young professionals to be culture-shaping, Christ-centered servant leaders in their various vocations. A partnership with Union University and Impact 360 Institute offers this unique, residentially-based Master of Christian Studies degree.

Get Connected

Find us online at impact360.org
Find us on Facebook at /impact360institute
Find us on Twitter at @impact360
Find us on Instagram at @impact360

John Basie knows college students and, perhaps more importantly, he knows their parents. *Your College Launch Story* is a great peek behind the scenes into the real-life conversations that surround both groups as young adults head off for their first taste of independence in college.

−GENE C. FANT, JR., Ph.D., author of *The Liberal Arts: A Student's Guide* (Crossway).

Our children need both roots to keep them firmly grounded and wings so they can soar. At no time in my life was this bittersweet truth more evident than the tearful ride home after my husband, John, and I left our oldest daughter at college, sixteen and a half hours from home! If we were to relive that experience again, I would hope we could read this book beforehand. Journeying with your child through this vital transition in life doesn't have to be an experience filled with anxiety, stress, fear, or uncertainty. Within the pages of this book are practical tools to guide you in this season, as you release your child to soar.

−TRUDY CATHY WHITE, Co-Founder, Lifeshape

College presents many challenges and opportunities for students and parents. In this concise, modern day fable, Dr. John Basie helps parents successfully launch their young adult students to college life. John has many years of real-life experience as an instructor, coach, and mentor. And I can testify that he knows what he is talking about. You see, he personally helped two of my own kids navigate this time in their lives, and I expect that I will trust him with a few more of my children sometime in the near future.

−DAVIS CARMAN, President, Apologia Educational Ministries

DEDICATION

In memory of my late mentor, David Gatewood,
who lived an authentic life *coram deo*
and showed me how to do the same
during a pivotal chapter of my own college story.

Contents

INTRODUCTION   11

CHAPTER 1: Understand the Deep Purpose   17
of a College Education

CHAPTER 2: Encourage Independence and   25
Stop Hovering

CHAPTER 3: Don't Freak Out   39

CHAPTER 4: Seek to Understand Your Student's   47
God-given, Unique Wiring

CHAPTER 5: Encourage Mentoring Relationships   57
Outside of Your Family

CHAPTER 6: Take the Long View   65

ENDNOTES   77

ABOUT THE AUTHOR   80

INTRODUCTION

This book is written for parents. More specifically, if you are the parent of a college-bound teenager or the parent of a current college student, this book is for you. Furthermore, you as the reader should know from the outset that I am a Christian; as such, I will be writing from that worldview perspective.

Although brief, this work has been a long time in the making . . . since 1992, in fact, when I began my journey into higher education, as a college freshman. Here, I've adapted my experiences into the stories of two families who have just launched their first-borns, both eighteen years old, into college. Within these pages lies a campus fable, with all characters being completely fictitious. Although no single character in the fable represents any one person with whom I've worked in the past, the characters do represent the diverse views, strengths, and challenges of the hundreds of students and parents I've had the privilege of walking alongside in my own journey as a professor, university dean, and professional life coach. Each chapter includes dialogue based the many conversations I've had with college students and parents over the years. Additionally, you will find a section at the end of each dialogue where I draw out implications for real life, based on my experience as well as other experts who have worked with college students.

Finally, each chapter concludes with a parent debrief section. This is where you have the opportunity dig deeper into your unique situation using the questions I have scripted. My hope is that you, as a parent of a college student or soon-to-be college student, will be able to use this resource as a guide to help you and your son or daughter script your ideal college launch story in a way that strengthens your family relationships over the next few years.

Before we dig into the story, let's get a little background information on the characters.

Kyle and His Parents

Kyle is freshman in college. Homeschooled through eighth grade, his parents enrolled him in public high school for ninth grade. There, he made good grades, served as senior class president, and was an outstanding athlete on the baseball team. As a committed Christian, Kyle has also been a faithful member of Fellowship of Christian Athletes since his ninth grade year, even serving as student president of his chapter during his junior year. By all accounts, he is a leader among his peers. Of the five universities he applied to, all five accepted him, and he chose his father's alma mater, following the same path his father traveled twenty-five years ago. It is a top-ranking university, although Kyle didn't choose it primarily for that reason; we'll learn more about Kyle's reasons as his story unfolds.

Kyle's father, Tom, is a highly successful corporate executive who works for a Fortune 500 company. He majored in business management, found a job as a sales associate in the technology sector, and has never looked back. Although Tom is grateful for his education, he says he owes a lot of his career success to the "quality job training" and college degree that landed him his first full-time position. He is also a committed Christian and has done the best he knows how in terms of balancing work and family life.

Tom works hard, very hard. He pulls sixty-hour work weeks regularly and sometimes, even longer. "It is what it is," he explains, because "that's what it takes to be at the top of the game." Tom has had many conversations with Kyle about how he'll really need to prepare to work just as hard if he wants to have the kind of life he has been used to, living in his parents' home.

Cindy is Tom's wife and Kyle's mother. She is loving and supportive to them both. While college-educated herself, Cindy simply sees college as "just the next step" to a happy and fulfilling life. That is Cindy's primary desire for Kyle—that he would be happy. She also wants all family members to be happy with each other all the time. Unlike Tom, who is highly competitive in work and in his conflict style, Cindy avoids conflict as much as possible; she just wants everyone to get along. Tom and Cindy have a good marriage overall, and Tom's father-son relationship with Kyle is fairly solid, too. Over the years, however, Tom's style of "pushing" to get what he thinks is best—in just about every decision—has led to a family dynamic where no one questions him or challenges his thinking . . . including Kyle. This family dynamic played a pretty big role in the way Kyle chose which university to attend.

Katie and Her Parents

Katie is a freshman at the same university as Kyle, and the two of them have been long-time friends. Their parents are also good friends. Katie's father, Jim, is also a highly accomplished businessman, having earned his B.A. and M.B.A. degrees from respected universities. Katie's mother, Sandra, is college-educated as well. Like Kyle's parents, Katie's parents are committed Christians and have sought to live Christ-centered lives at work, home, and in their recreational time. Unlike Kyle's parents, however, Jim and Sandra believe a college education isn't primarily about getting a degree, getting a job, or being happy. They do agree, however, that those things are very important for Katie, and that her education will certainly help her in meeting those goals.

So although they agree that having a recognized credential will help to make Katie a happier person, Jim and Sandra maintain that those benefits are not fundamental to a university education. They hold the view that becoming educated means becoming a certain *kind* of person; namely, a wise and virtuous person. They've agreed that whatever major Katie chooses will be her choice, so long as she is taking her core classes in the arts and sciences seriously.

We've established there are also some fairly stark differences in personalities between the two couples. Unlike Tom, Jim doesn't appear to be such a relentless hard-driver in his work. To be sure, Jim is a hard worker, regularly putting in fifty hours a week and occasionally more when he travels. But there is a noticeable difference in the way that Jim thinks about his work; he approaches his work primarily as a way to use his gifts productively in the world. "How can I use my God-given strengths to make a difference today?" That question guides Jim's way of working.

Now, regarding Jim and Sandra's marriage: While they are happy overall, their marriage looks significantly different from Tom and Cindy's. Jim tends to be more laid back in his approach to decision-making, preferring to defer either to Sandra or to the family majority. Sandra's personality is actually more of a "take-charge" style than Jim's, and always has been ever since they began dating in college. In fact, she used to be unpredictably intense, sometimes blowing up at Jim and other friends when things didn't quite go her way or when she was confronted with a problem she couldn't solve quickly. As a responsible, structured, planner-type of personality, Sandra expects to follow through on what she says she's going to do and expects others to do the same. Although she has learned to control this intensity most of the time and channel it productively, it came out more in a negative way during Katie's college search process. Now that Katie has chosen her university and is in school, Sandra finds herself grieving Katie's departure from home and is reverting back to that unpleasant person more often than she or Katie would like.

ONE

UNDERSTAND THE DEEP PURPOSE OF A COLLEGE EDUCATION

J im, Sandra, Tom, and Cindy have been friends for a long time. Having attended the same church, lived in the same neighborhood for ten years, and with children (Katie and Kyle) being the same age, it was natural for them to get together fairly often. On this particular evening, Jim and Sandra were at Tom and Cindy's home for a late October backyard barbeque. As Tom grilled the steaks, the four friends struck up a conversation about how Katie and Kyle were doing in their first semester at college.

Sandra was first to express how happy she was that Kyle and Katie had decided to go to the same university. "I'm just so excited that they can help and support each other right now. Isn't it just fantastic?" she said.

Cindy quickly agreed. "Oh, I know, I'm so thankful for that, too. That university seems like such a big, scary place to me, and it makes me feel a whole lot better to know that they are both there together."

Tom quickly cut in, "I'm sure they will watch out for each other, Cindy. My concern about Kyle right now is that he isn't focused. He still doesn't know what he wants to do with his life, so that means he's not sure about a major, either. I've told him repeatedly that he should major in business if he wants to get a good job right after college, but I'm not sure he is really hearing me. The whole thing is just frustrating to me. When I went to college, I knew what I wanted; I dove in, and never looked back. And to this day, I have no regrets."

"That's my husband," Cindy quickly added with a playful look at Tom. "Always certain."

"And," Jim chimed in with a grin on his face, "always certain that others should be as certain as he is."

Tom chuckled as he replied, "It's gotten us this far, hasn't it? Why should I consider any other way?" The steaks were finished grilling, and the four friends chuckled as they moved over to the backyard patio to eat. As they ate, the conversation about their kids continued, but took on a new texture as they began to discuss why college is essential these days.

Sandra spoke up and said, "Well, I know Katie needs to be educated, but sometimes I just wish she had chosen a place closer to home."

Tom confidently said, "Yeah, four hours makes for a long drive all right. But it's a great institution. I credit that university with helping me to get where I am today. Cindy and I definitely see the importance of a college education for Kyle. How can anyone these days get a job without at least a bachelor's degree? That is the main idea behind a college education, right? To get training for the real world of work, so that you can get a good job and begin a successful career?"

"Well, uh, I'm not so sure about that, Tom," Jim politely pushed back.

"Really?" Tom responded with surprise. "And you even have a M.B.A.—more education than I have. What do you think *is* the main point of a college education?"

Jim continued, "Even though I'm on the business side of things now, I see the value of my liberal arts education each and every day in my work, because I can see how business, at its best, is a very humane activity. Even when business isn't at its best, because of my education in the humanities, I have a deep understanding of what it should be like—and it has everything to do with human flourishing. So an education is more than just a ticket to a high-paying job; it is a way of being human. My double major in Bible and philosophy, coupled with a minor in business management, has helped me to see that. Having that blend of disciplines helped me to see how God's Word and his world are intimately connected. To me, the activity of business itself is a way of honoring God through filling and subduing the earth—an insight that daily shapes my goals, and how I deal with people and make decisions. I want Katie to have a similar experience so that she, too, will see how God's Word and his world are tightly bound together. I don't expect her to study the exact same things in the exact same way I did; rather, I want her to be able to see that her work—the work she chooses, and the way she chooses to do it—is deeply connected to the image of God in her."

Tom didn't respond at first. He was thinking about what Jim had just said about God's Word and world being "tightly bound together." He was also caught off-guard by how articulate Jim had been in expressing the connection between the idea that human beings bear God's image and how it reflects in the work that they do. It wasn't the kind of comment that anyone would be able to make without having thought it through pretty well.

"You know, Jim," Tom said, three steak bites later, "I don't know why, but the way you said what you just did about work, being an image-bearer, and God's Word and world made me feel uncomfortable."

"Sorry, Tom," Jim quickly replied. "I certainly didn't mean to . . ." At that moment, Tom held up his hand and motioned for Jim to stop his apology mid-sentence.

"No, not at all," Tom reassured him. "It made me feel uncomfortable in a good way, at least that's what my intuition is telling me. You see, it's not often I'm that quiet for that long when friends are around, so the fact that your explanation gave me pause is telling me that I need to sit up and pay attention to something here. Now, can you help me understand your point more clearly?"

"Sure thing," Jim said, with an energetic tone. "Think of it this way. If God created everything there is, including us, and if He had a purpose in creating us and placing us on this earth, and if He went so far as to say 'finish the work I've begun here, and make it as good as you possibly can,'[1] then wouldn't you want to find the place—or the calling—in which you could make the greatest contribution to that work?"

Tom shrugged and agreed reluctantly. "Well, sure, who wouldn't want that?" He was beginning to see that Jim's entire way of understanding the meaning of work itself was far more profound than his own, and he felt a bit defensive at that moment. After a brief pause in the conversation, Tom said, "I guess I've always just seen my career as one opportunity after another . . . and I hate turning down good opportunities. Anyway, my way of seeing work has helped set my family on solid financial footing in ways that wouldn't otherwise have been possible. I'm only fifty, and I really don't have to work for the money anymore. And I'd like Kyle to be in the same or even better financial position when he's my age. I don't want him to have to struggle the way we did when Cindy and were first starting out."

"I can't argue with that, Tom," Jim replied. "We hope Katie never has to worry for anything, either. We've been able to provide well for her, and even though she is accustomed to our lifestyle, we've tried to teach her over the years that these material things we have are blessings to be sure and that we can enjoy them. But we've also been very intentional in teaching her that material things don't last. I don't care if you have two million dollars saved up in cash—even that could be gone in the blink of an eye if our economy really tanked. Besides, it's quite possible she'll marry a guy whose career can't support the lifestyle that we have."

> If God created everything there is, including us, and if He had a purpose in creating us . . . then wouldn't you want to find the place—or the calling—in which you could make the greatest contribution to that work?

"I guess that's something I've never really thought about before," Cindy admitted.

Jim continued, "The moral of the story is simply this: Money, stuff, and the comfort they give us are great. I love my house, our nice cars, and watching my retirement nest egg grow. There's nothing wrong with any of those, but they aren't the *main thing*. How could they be, *if stuff by its very nature is only temporary?*

Tom was visibly unsettled. "I don't know, Jim. If money isn't part of the equation, why then should we work?"

Jim replied, "I didn't *quite* say that money wasn't a part of the equation. Think about it this way: Our generation—the boomers—in general have gone about their work as if the paycheck was the only thing that really mattered. That thinking is basically a 'survival-of-the-fittest" view of work—that we work only for the sake of attaining security. That perspective says we ought to accrue as much stuff as possible during our working lives so that we can have more security. The more security we have, the happier we will be. While there is some connection between physical security and happiness, it isn't the whole picture if we're truly made in God's image. If we're made in His image, then we're made *for* something far greater than mere survival. The security that material possessions provide can't possibly be the main thing we're working for; if that were the case, then how are we really more dignified in our work than any wild animal scrounging around for food and shelter? If material things and financial security aren't the central purpose of work, then what is? And if the purpose of work is something *more* than setting a secure financial footing for our families, then shouldn't a solid college education be *more* than just job preparation for our adult kids?"

Tom responded, "I'm not saying I'm totally convinced, but you've given me and Cindy a lot to think about, Jim. Maybe I'll process this for a while and get back to you." The conversation quickly shifted to other things, and the four friends finished their meal and enjoyed the remainder of the evening together. They agreed to have dinner together at least once more before Kyle and Katie came home for Christmas break.

Implications for Real Life: Pursuing God's Call vs. Survival of the Fittest

What's the main difference in the way that Kyle's and Katie's parents view the purpose of a college education? It's pretty simple: Kyle's parents assume that a college education's main value is the long-term financial security that it should help their son achieve. Katie's parents see the main value of a college education as a means for her to become more of the kind of person God designed her to be—namely a Christ-centered, virtuous person who is seeking to discern God's unique calling on her life. To be sure, they believe it is very important for Katie to find a job following college that provides sufficient financial security for her needs. With some diligence and hard work on her part, they know she can land that first job, but they also know that she will experience more holistic growth as God's image-bearer if she keeps the deepest purposes of her education in mind as she finishes college.

At the end of the day, Katie's parents have a deeper and fuller understanding of what a college education is meant to be than Kyle's parents do. They understand that the best of a college education is one where the whole person is developed, one that addresses their intellect, character, and the physical self. Furthermore, they hold that it is a mistake to view college as a mere commodity.[2] I cannot underscore this point enough. There is a wildly popular but sadly reductionistic view of education out there that many refer to as "vocational training." This view of education says that the only really worthy outcome of education is practical work that one can be paid to do. At this point in our campus fable, that is Tom's view of a college education's main value. And, in my experience, that is what most parents assume is the main value for their sons and daughters.

Let me be clear before I go on. I am not against practical education. In fact, I am very much for it. As a professional career coach for millennial generation students, I have worked

> The best of a college education is one where the whole person is developed, one that addresses their intellect, character, and the physical self.

with many young people whose God-given learning styles are more hands-on, learning-by-doing than it is sitting in a traditional classroom and reading scores of lengthy scholarly texts. In many cases, this kind of student is uniquely gifted to do superb hands-on work to God's glory such as auto mechanics, construction, or cosmetology in ways that more traditional learners simply aren't capable of. A truly Christian understanding of work says that every calling is a sacred calling. Vocational education at its best "is one that understands the role of God's call on our lives whether we are professional Christians or clergy or lay persons who view the work of our hands as a direct gift from God."[3] Even more practically-oriented hands-on learners are better prepared when they understand at a basic level how their work fits within the broader context of the world God created. Why are they better prepared when they understand this? Because it helps them catch a glimpse into their life purpose and calling.

Katie's parents understand that college, if she truly applies herself, will help her to discern where she experiences grace through her own unique set of gifts and strengths. Why grace? Because it is intimately tied to how we discern God's call on our lives. As author Andy Crouch has pointed out, "the single best question for discerning our calling . . . is 'Where do you experience grace—divine multiplication that far exceeds your efforts?' Grace is not a shortcut around our effort; it is the divine blessing on efforts that are undertaken in dependence and trust on God."[4]

PARENT DEBRIEF

As you go through the following debrief questions, please remember that some will be more relevant to your situation than others.

1 If you went to college, think back for a moment to your freshman orientation. What can you remember about your motivation for being there? If you could go back in time and have a talk with yourself—your 18-year-old self who is just starting college—what would you say?

2 What do you believe the core purpose of a college education is? What does your student believe, in this regard?

3 After reading through the conversation between Jim and Tom, where do you find your views of college challenged or stretched in some way?

4 What are your thoughts about the claim that every calling is a sacred calling from God?

TWO

ENCOURAGE INDEPENDENCE AND STOP HOVERING

As parents, one of your biggest temptations will be to continue the same relational patterns with your college-age child that were in place while he or she grew up in your home and under your supervision. This is particularly true as it comes to keeping tabs on your now fully grown, adult child. And yes, your eighteen-year-old is an adult . . . although you may think otherwise. You have a choice, Mom and Dad. To grasp this point, let's now turn our attention to Katie and Kyle, who attend the same college and have kept up their friendship.

"Hey Kyle, how's it going?" asked an energetic, glad-to-be alive Katie. The two friends typically caught up once a week with each other over a couple of lattes at the campus café in the Davis Student Center.

"Okay," muttered Kyle. "Could be worse."

"Well, there's my optimist friend!" Katie teased. "Seriously, what's eating at you?"

"All right, I guess you're not gonna leave it alone until I spill it, huh?" conceded Kyle.

"You know me too well," smiled Katie, settling in with another sip of her latte.

"Here's what I don't get," explained Kyle. "Why do my Mom and Dad expect me to text them and talk to them on the phone just as often now that I'm at college as when I was living at home? I mean, I think I should keep up with them, but seriously, I didn't expect to have to give them a play-by-play of what I'm doing all day, every day. I understood why they wanted it to be this way while I was still in high school, but I thought things would change when I went to college. Do your parents have that same expectation?"

"They used to," sighed Katie. "I don't know how to compare my situation to yours, but what my parents and I do now works pretty well for us."

"So, what *do* you all do?" probed Kyle.

"We agreed to talk on the phone once a week for the first semester. Between calls, we don't really text each other." Katie explained.

"And why is that?" Kyle was on the edge of his seat, in disbelief that his good friend had such a different scenario than his own. He was somewhat envious.

"Because . . . " Katie patiently replied, "this past summer, my parents and I realized that there were certain things that made sense for us when I was in high school that probably weren't going to work well now that I'm in college. We had a series of intentional discussions about those things, and this was one of the areas we identified as needing to change as I made that transition. More specifically, we don't text each other because my parents know that they have to let go of me as I get fully immersed into my new home here at school. They know I can't really build a meaningful community here if they are always following me around on my phone."

"Wow!" Kyle exclaimed. "That's . . . really great." He was having a hard time being happy for her; it dawned on him how intentional Katie and her parents had been with regard to her college transition . . . and how unintentional Kyle and his parents had been about his.

"But hang on, there's more," Katie interjected, sensing Kyle's disengagement from the conversation.

"Oh, yippee. I'd really like to hear more about how great and forward-thinking your amazing parents are," Kyle snorted, sarcastically.

Kyle's tone stung Katie. "Now wait a second, that's not fair," she continued. "You asked, so I told you, right? There is something else worth pointing out here. We set our communication up this way as much for my benefit as for theirs. They weren't the only ones texting me all throughout the day in high school; I was texting them a whole lot, too. I love my parents a whole lot, and I knew that I would probably lean on them too much if we didn't set up this once-a-week call schedule. In high school, when I got into some kind of jam I couldn't solve, I would just text or call my mom and she would tell me what to do to solve the problem."

Kyle was tracking with Katie. He nodded his head in full agreement. "Yeah, I know what you mean. I don't like asking people I don't know well for help. It's just easier and more comfortable for me to reach out to Dad to help me with my math homework, or Mom if I have a question about a paper or something. Come to think of it, she's already helped me with two of my essays for my English literature class."

"See, that's what I'm talking about!" Katie explained. "I've had a couple of papers to turn in, too. My first impulse was to send my rough drafts home to my mom to get her to proof them for me. But then, I remembered what we had discussed about communication and learning to become more independent, and . . . " Katie's voiced trailed off.

"And what?" Kyle insisted.

Katie continued, with tears welling up in her eyes. "And I just didn't expect it to be this difficult. I mean, I'm loving college so far, and I'm really glad I'm here. But I love my parents, like, a lot. And I miss them being nearby."

Kyle was eager to offer comfort. "Sorry, Katie. I had no idea it had been this difficult for you. It sounds like you have such a great relationship with your parents. I'm curious, though, why didn't you just stay back home and go to the local university there? That way, you could've kept living with them the same as before."

"Fair question," explained Katie. "And actually, we discussed that. I even applied there, and was accepted. But when it came down to making a decision, the coach we were using asked us some really good questions that helped all of us see that me staying local for my college education would not have been the best choice."

"Whoa, wait a sec!" Kyle was confused by her answer. "You were talking to a coach about colleges? You've never been an athlete— were you thinking about being a walk-on or something?"

"No, not that kind of coach," replied Katie patiently. "We hired a life coach who specializes in helping high school students and their parents transition into college. They help make the process smoother."

"Oh, okay. I get it. Yeah, a life coach. I think I've heard my older sister talk about a life coach who has helped her with figuring out how to balance her full-time job with her family, church, and everything else she's doing without going completely insane."

"Yep, that's right. In fact, the reason we hired a coach to help our family through my transition is that I heard your sister talk about how helpful her coach has been to her in learning how to keep all of those things going, how to do them well, and still enjoy life. I asked my parents about hiring a coach to help us through the college transition, and they agreed because they saw the value. I also think it helped that they remembered how poorly my older brother launched into college three years ago, and they knew at some level they contributed to his less-than-stellar transition. So it didn't take much convincing on my part."

"That's cool. I wish I'd thought about that myself—that kind of person could've helped my parents and me," Kyle mused.

"Yeah, it sounds like it.," Katie agreed. "But don't you think a coach could still help you and your parents, right now?"

"Probably," Kyle admitted reluctantly. "If it were someone I knew, or at least could learn to trust pretty quickly. I just don't know if my parents would be open to it. Besides, I'm already here, and my folks and I are already in a routine. I don't like it, but it's just easier not to rock the boat."

"That sounds like your Mom talking, Kyle," observed Katie. "I've been around your family enough to know that your Dad's very strong personality helps him get his way, and your Mom, like you just said, makes sure not to rock the boat."

Katie's observation made Kyle chuckle, realizing that someone else outside of his family could see the relational dynamics. "You know that's right," he remarked quietly. " It's always been this way, and it's hard for me to see how it could be different."

Katie's eyes opened wide. "Exactly!" she cried. "Sometimes, it takes a trustworthy, objective person who can ask good questions to help us see how it *can* be different. There were some key things that my parents and I didn't see at all on our own, because we have been living with each other for so long, operating with the same family rhythms for years."

"Like what?" Kyle leaned in.

Katie's answered without hesitation. "First, we didn't see the ways in which we were stuck," she explained. "And I mean things like relational dynamics, work habits, and ways of communicating that were less than healthy for my parents and me. Second, we weren't seeing my potential in some key areas that could really be developed in the college years. And third, I didn't have any compelling vision for what my life during college and beyond could really be. I know I've been a Christian for a long time, and have grown up in the church, but honestly, being driven by a God-sized life vision just wasn't a thing for me at all until we started meeting with our coach."

Now fully engaged, Kyle was hanging on Katie's every word. "Wow, it sounds like this coach made a huge difference in your life."

"She did," Katie answered, again without hesitation. "But not because she told us what to do."

"Really?" inquired Kyle.

Nodding emphatically, Katie underscored how strongly she felt about this point. "Yes. Really. The main reason our coach was so good was that she asked powerful questions that helped us to identify our own best way of moving forward. And, the coolest part is that it was so natural for her to invite the Holy Spirit into the coaching process to show me and my parents where God wanted us to go, not just where we thought we wanted to go."

"Wow. That's *way* different from the way my parents and I did things," Kyle replied.

"How so?" Katie inquired with a quizzical look.

"Well, for starters," Kyle answered, "it never occurred to me that there was another way to think about my time in college. From what you've shared so far, you make it sound like *you actively chose* to come to this university."

Katie's eyebrows were up as she nodded her head in excitement. "That's exactly right! But only as a result of stepping back and seeing what was going on with my parents and me."

Kyle, still sitting forward, nodded too. "Right, that's what I'm seeing is so different between our two situations. It's kind of weird."

"What does that mean?" Katie asked.

"Think about it, Katie. We're both here, at this institution, beginning our college careers. From an outsider's perspective, we both got the same result—acceptance to a respected university. But you're here because *you actively chose* this place. I'm here because of the family momentum that I just went along with. It was the path of least resistance. I never really thought about what it would mean to be an active chooser in the college search process; I just never questioned anything along the way, really. My parents—mostly my Dad—have always talked about me coming here because he did, and I thought . . . "

Katie interrupted him before he could finish, "And you just thought that's how things worked for everyone."

"Yes," Kyle sighed. "Now, my problem, I'm just now realizing, is that I really don't know what I'm doing here. I've not bought in. I feel like the decision was made for me, and now I just have to live with it—kind of like the way I just have to live with my parents texting me all day long and expecting me to respond to each one within minutes."

"Maybe," Katie conceded, half-heartedly. "Or maybe you're playing the victim."

"What?" demanded Kyle, put off by his friend's direct approach.

Softening her tone, Katie tried to reassure her friend. "Oh, come on, Kyle. You trust me, right? How much do you really want to know why I said that?"

"Yes, I trust you . . . sorry," Kyle sheepishly replied. "Please, keep going. I do want to hear why you think I'm pretending to be a victim."

"Now wait, Kyle. I didn't say 'pretending,'" Katie clarified. "I said *playing*. Playing the victim means that you're saying 'woe is me' about your circumstances in order to gain sympathy from others. In your case, it sounds like you're always complaining about how your outside world is set against you in ways that you can't control, when in reality you have more control than you think. It's an attention-seeking behavior that you may not even realize you engage in."

"You mean I'm doing it unconsciously?" probed Kyle.

"It's possible. That's all I'm saying. You'll have to think about it and decide for yourself," Katie said in a gentle, yet confident way.

"Huh, I've never thought about this before," Kyle admitted. "Although, now that I'm going over this in my head, I think I'm recognizing that my Mom does this a lot."

"Yeah," Katie agreed reluctantly. "I was kind of wondering about that. I've seen her do it sometimes when I've been at your house."

Kyle offered an explanation. "Maybe it's one way she deals with my Dad's strong personality. She refuses to lean into any conflict— she's so scared to challenge anyone, now that I think about it."

Katie circled back to where the conversation began. "I wonder how all of this is related to the constant texting you're getting from them both. More importantly, I'm wondering what *you* are going to choose to do about it, Kyle. Something my life coach helped me understand as I was getting ready to launch into college is that our circumstances, including how people treat us—yes, including our parents—are usually a result of two things: What we create, and what we allow."

Kyle was encouraged. "This is really, really helpful stuff, Katie. Looks like I need to take more responsibility in what I'm creating and allowing in my life. But what about my Mom?"

"What do you mean, what about her?" Katie asked.

"She seems to need me, like, too much." Kyle said emphatically.

"In what way?"

"Okay, that's easy," Kyle responded. "For instance, just last night, Mom called me right when I was on my way out to play a game of ultimate with the guys. She'd texted me right before, say-

> Our circumstances, including how people treat us—yes, including our parents—are usually a result of two things: What we create, and what we allow.

ing it was urgent, so I picked up when the phone buzzed. When we started talking, I could tell she had been crying. She's all upset about my younger brother, Brian, going off the rails again at school. He's been messing up his sophomore year in high school; he hasn't made good decisions regarding friends, and yesterday Brian and some of his friends were busted at school for drugs."

"Oh, that's gotta be tough . . . and embarrassing for both of them." Katie empathized.

"Yeah, especially for Mom. She's always been pretty protective of Brian, for whatever reason. Mom knows Brian and I are pretty tight, and I understand him, so she's usually relied on me more than my Dad for help with him when he gets into a jam."

"Hmm . . . sounds like that puts you in a pretty awkward place," Katie said.

"Yeah, I guess it does. But, this is the family dynamic we've had for so long now that nobody questions it, not even Dad. In fact, I think he might be relieved that Mom comes to me instead of him about stuff related to Brian," Kyle explained.

"Wow," Katie said. "No pressure or anything! So much for you just being a son . . . you have to be a Dad to your brother, too? Your father needs to be the father!

Kyle let out a big sigh. "Yeah, I guess you're right, but, like I said, this has been the family pattern for so long now that no one questions it."

Katie wasn't convinced. She looked at him with one raised eyebrow and said firmly, but gently, "You do."

"Yeah, well, maybe," Kyle conceded in a half-committed tone. "I question it privately, when I think about it, but I try not to think about it. Besides, even if I raised the issue with my parents, I don't think it would go well. Best I can tell, they haven't really had a good discussion about this issue themselves. It's just kind of the thing they're used to now, and they just go with it."

Katie pressed in. "So you're okay to allow this family dynamic to continue? Remember what were just saying about how our circumstances are a result of . . . "

Kyle finished her sentence before she could get the words out. "Yes, I get it . . . what we create, or what we allow. So yes, I am allowing this to continue, in some sense."

"But why?" Katie asked.

"Honestly," Kyle patiently explained, "because it's easier than upsetting the applecart. I don't like conflict, and I'd rather just see if the crazy way that we deal with my brother just works itself out somehow, without me having to confront my parents."

Katie kept pressing. "Seriously, Kyle? You think this is somehow going to work itself out without any intentionality on your part? How many years has this been going on?"

"Three, at least," Kyle said.

"Well, that's a pretty much an ingrained pattern. Let me see if I understand this: You're okay with 'just seeing how it goes' and allowing your independence—what should be growing adult independence—to keep taking a beating until it 'just works itself out somehow?' What if it doesn't just work itself out? What will that look like next year in college, and the year after that, and the year after that? Fast forward to the day when you find a great girl and get married. Do you think being married will somehow magically fix this craziness in your family? Wake up! This is going to follow you right into your marriage if you don't do something about it, starting now. How will your new bride feel when she wakes up one day and realizes that her mother-in-law leans *way* too heavily on you for something that ought to handled mostly in their own family unit? Also, I'm beginning to wonder what else your Mom might be too dependent on you for."

Kyle had disgruntled look on his face, as Katie's implication gave him a reaction of disgust and surprise. "Ugh. I've never thought about it that way before. I've just never thought that far ahead on what things could look like for me. When you put it that way, it could be a pretty miserable existence."

> Independence, properly understood and practiced, is essential for a college student's growth.

Katie nodded in agreement. "Yes, but it doesn't have to be. Kyle, I'm not saying you can't help with your brother; clearly, you can and should . . . at some level. But for you to basically shoulder the responsibility that your father ought to be taking just isn't . . . "

Again, Kyle finished Katie's sentence. ". . . healthy. I know, it isn't. So I guess I need to have a conversation with my parents about this."

Since both had a class to attend, the two friends parted ways until the following week.

Implications for real life: The Easy Path vs. the Growth Path

The main theme we see coming up in this conversation between Katie and Kyle is not texting or dysfunctional family dynamics—but those are a part of the problem, for sure. From a student perspective, the main theme is *independence*. Independence, properly understood and practiced, is essential for a college student's growth. Granted, not everyone grows at the same rate, but personal, spiritual, and social growth must happen in key ways during the college years. What is independence? It is the ability to be self-directed and free from unhealthy emotional dependency on others.[5] Someone with healthy independence will be able to make decisions and complete tasks without always needing others to step in to do it for him.

For years now, I've personally witnessed a decrease in healthy independence in college students. The proliferation of mobile phones, unlimited texting plans, and having access to most or all of their students' email (including college-issued email) and social media accounts now allow parents to follow their students around wherever they go, even if they aren't physically present—a phenomenon that some have referred to as "drone parenting."[6] And what I've seen is backed up by what other experts in the field are seeing on a national scale. Many college students send and receive over one hundred texts per day.[7] Not all of those texts are going from parent to student and vice-versa, but it does show how attached college students are to their smart phones. And, from my personal experience, far too many parents are just as attached to their phones. They see the mobile phone as their child's lifeline, what some researchers have called "the world's longest umbilical cord."[8]

To strengthen my point about declining independence in the college student population, more and more college students are seeking professional counseling help for issues that the average student twenty years ago would have worked through autonomously. It is now all too common for experienced university faculty to have students falling apart emotionally in their offices because of a low grade. Instead of rising to the challenge and saying, "I need to work harder to earn a decent grade," the students' attitudes these days compared to two or three decades ago is basically "make the course easier," or "tell me exactly what I need to know so there is zero ambiguity for me." This indicates a lack of student resilience, which often stems from a lack of experience in making decisions or working through problems on one's own.[9]

> To what extent are you encouraging your college-bound young adult to be independent?

Independence is an essential ingredient for emotional intelligence growth, which is key for success beyond college. Author and millennial generation expert Tim Elmore often tells students that success in college is about seventy-five percent cognitive intelligence (or IQ) and twenty-five percent emotional intelligence (EQ), while success in life is just the opposite. Seventy-five percent of life success depends on strong emotional intelligence, which also includes self-awareness, self-management, social awareness, and relationship management.[10]

Katie and Kyle's conversation is a version of a dialogue that I've heard students having—or that I've had with students myself—over the years. It's a serious problem, Mom and Dad, and you may not understand exactly how serious it is. I'm not saying that this is definitely *your specific* problem, because I have no idea what your situation is. But I am asking the question: To what extent are you encouraging your college-bound young adult to be independent?

PARENT DEBRIEF

As you go through the following debrief questions, please remember that some will be more relevant to your situation than others.

1 What were your main takeaways from Kyle and Katie's conversation? What surprised you?

2 On a scale of one to ten, with ten being "I do this regularly," how often do you allow your student to struggle rather than immediately solving his or her problem?

3 In what ways do you find yourself seeking to solve your student's problems for her or him? What are some patterns you can identify? Be specific. If you can't think of anything, what would it take for you to ask your student?

4 On average, how many text conversations per week are you having with your son or daughter? Of those, how many do you initiate? How many does your student initiate?

5 On average, how many phone calls per week do you have with your son or daughter? Of those, how many do you initiate? How many does your student initiate?

6 What are some areas of life where you may have become too emotionally dependent on your son or daughter? Be specific. If you can't think of anything, what would it take for you to ask him/her?

THREE

DON'T FREAK OUT

When Kyle and Katie met at the Davis Student Center for their lattes the following week, the mood tables had turned quite a bit. This time, Kyle was upbeat and chipper while Katie was struggling to keep her usual sense of optimism. Kyle did all the talking as the two friends waited in line for the barista to take their order.

He launched right into an update. "So, on Sunday I had that conversation with my parents about my brother Brian and how it was negatively impacting my independence. It was hard, but it went much, much better than I ever would have thought. The 'win' is that they are open to talking more about it. So I'll take that for now."

Katie, trying to smile and be gracious, unenthusiastically said, "That really great, Kyle. It's a huge step forward."

Without missing a beat, Kyle moved on in his reporting to her. "I got my English lit essay back. I did better than I thought I would: *B*-plus! Dr. Moser said the class average was a *C*, so I felt pretty good about that."

Katie, unimpressed, responded in an uncharacteristically sarcastic way. "Wow. You're a genius. And so is the professor. I guess the good Dr. Moser is an expert in math as well as English—he figured out that *C* means average."

"Whoa . . . what's with you today?" Kyle demanded. "Something's gotten under your skin?"

"Sorry, Kyle. You didn't deserve that." Katie's face was proof of her disappointment with how she had just treated her good friend.

"No worries," Kyle said without hesitation. "So what's up? You want to tell me what's going on?"

Katie sighed. "Yeah—as crummy as I feel and as much as I don't want to talk about it, I know I need to. And, I trust you, so here goes."

"Great, I'm all ears," Kyle reassured her.

"Okay, I'll cut right to the chase: Mom and I had a pretty big fight on the phone this morning right before my 9:00 a.m. class."

"About what?"

"Apparently, about almost everything in my life right now. She was freaking out in my ear on the phone," explained Katie, with intensity.

Kyle pressed for more context. "Freaking out? What about?"

Using her fingers, Katie ticked off a laundry list. "Well, first, I told her on the phone this morning is that I'm currently making a *C* in biology. That really rocked her world. In high school, I never made anything below a *B+*, so this was a real shock to her system. Never mind the fact that I'm disappointed in myself."

"For sure," Kyle affirmed.

Katie continued, "Second, she found out this morning that I'm not planning to come home for fall break. She really flipped out about that, too. She had made all these plans for our family that hinged on my being there. Some of what she was telling me she had planned was really cool stuff, too. We just had never communicated about my plans, and we both had different expectations for what my fall break from school would be. She wants me to be home with the family, and I want to experience fall break with my new college friends."

"That's what I'm doing—going on a fall break road trip with a group of guys," Kyle shared. "I can't wait."

"I'm jealous," Katie replied, smiling just a bit. "I'm probably going to give in this time and just go home. But there's one more thing that set Mom off. I told her that I'm looking for a part-time job because my expenses have been a bit more than we anticipated. They've helped as much as they can financially, and told me before I left that they wouldn't be able to do anything else."

Kyle was confused. "Wait—so then why is she upset that you're getting a job? You're not asking your parents for more money or anything."

"Exactly!" Katie exclaimed. "Of the three topics that she's upset over, this is the one that bothers me the most. She can't offer more money, but she's yelling at me that I'm wasting my time working when I should be focused on my studies. It's not fair. Okay, I go out with friends on occasion and that takes spending money, but I don't spend a ton on that. Where I'm falling short is on basics, like money for books and laundry."

"Wow," exclaimed a surprised Kyle. "After our conversation last week, I'm a bit surprised to hear how your mother chose to speak to you this morning."

Katie nodded. "Yeah, well, even healthy families have their issues. This is one of ours. Our life coach spotted it fairly early on in the coaching process late last spring after I had just been accepted to several colleges."

"Spotted what, exactly?"

"My mother's tendency to get freaked out by things that happen outside of her control or her plan, and then to 'whack' whomever she perceives to be at fault. I don't mean that she physically whacks anyone—I mean she basically tears into the other person with sharp words and blame. Sometimes she will even use crying as a manipulation tool."

"That's enough to make a person feel lousy," replied an empathetic Kyle.

"It does," Katie said. "But do you know what feels worse? When she gives one of us the silent treatment."

"Oh, wow. I hate that, too—it doesn't accomplish anything," Kyle replied, wincing.

> No one's perfect, and there's certainly no perfect parent.

"Don't get me wrong. I love my mom and we have great relationship. And she's really improved in this area over the summer, working with our coach. But change comes hard, and there are still times when she freaks out and once again, I get whacked."

"Yeah, I get it about change not being easy. But I'm still surprised. I've always seen your parents as the near-perfect couple, and your Mom has always been so kind and hospitable when I've been in your home," Kyle observed.

Katie quickly agreed with Kyle's assessment, but added her own thoughts. "Yes, she is kind and hospitable. She is a fantastic Mom! But no one's perfect, and there's certainly no perfect parent. And admittedly, I've given her my share of challenges as a teenager. What I think I'm learning to do now is actively put myself in her shoes when she gets all huffy with me and, instead of withdrawing or whacking her back, leaning into her and trusting the relationship that we have. That way, I'm able to get past all the emotional stuff she's throwing my way so that I can really 'see' what's going on with her."

Kyle was blown away, his eyes wide open. "That sounds really mature, as in, like, 'so-mature-that-no-eighteen-year-old-I-know-does-this' type mature."

"Well," said Katie laughed, "It doesn't always go so well, like this morning. But I'm making a concerted effort. And, to her credit, she's improved in this area and is continuing to work hard not to freak out on me when she experiences a loss of control or change of plans."

"Is there anything I can do to help you in all this?" Kyle asked.

"Just be there for me in moments like this," Katie replied, gratefully. "As hard as it was at first to talk about it, it got easier after I got rolling. And, I feel a lot better now. I'm really glad that you pulled this out of me this morning—you're a great friend."

Kyle smiled and said, "Any time, Katie."

Implications for Real Life

Every young person, especially in a time of transition like college life, wants to feel loved by their parents. This means, among other things, that parents will need to act in a way that tells the student "No matter what, you are safe with us. We respect you. And, we value you." But that's not always so easy, especially when parents are used to "freaking out" as a way of responding to bad news the student shares.

The two friends' conversation this time focused on the ongoing challenge Katie has had with her mother's emotionally intense reactions, or

> Every young person, especially in a time of transition like college life, wants to feel loved by their parents.

her "freak-outs." In this case, Sandra's reactions were highlighted as the problem, and Katie was portrayed as an innocent victim of her mother's wrath. While that does happen, I realize it isn't always the case. Very often, a student makes a bad choice or directly defies or deceives parents in some way. Whether or not your student has done something wrong isn't really the point; the point is that if you struggle with keeping your emotions in check with your student when he or she shares something disappointing, your relationship with him or her is at risk. It may have been at risk for quite some time already.

Trust me on this. I've coached too many students who have shared that they can't tell their parents something important because they fear they will once again get "whacked" in some way, by one or both. In other words, they don't feel safe, respected, or valued. It isn't that most students don't want to be held accountable, at least not in my experience; and it isn't that they don't want a relationship with their parents. In fact, every student I've ever taught or coached, deep down wants a meaningful relationship with both parents. But if a student has become accustomed to getting "whacked," then what do you think he or she has learned to do? Avoid the pain of the "whack." So, typically what that looks like is the student choosing to not share some really important things with parents. What that amounts to is hiding certain things from them because the student perceives that it won't be safe to share.

I'm not saying, parents, that you shouldn't have hard conversations with your student or hold him or her accountable in appropriate ways. Your student, however, is now an adult—yes, *an adult*. As hard as that may be for you to perceive and believe, it is the truth. He or she may be an immature adult, but that doesn't change the reality that your student is no longer a little boy or little girl.

That being said, he or she is going through some tremendous changes in this transition to college. Do you remember what it was like for you? You may have experienced all kinds of self-doubt, fears, and disappointments. You also had some memorable successes. It's no different for your son or daughter. No matter what, he or she wants that relationship with you. So in those moments when you're tempted to freak out, remember that your son or daughter is an image-bearer who wants and needs to tell you something important.

> In those moments when you're tempted to freak out, remember that your son or daughter is an image-bearer who wants and needs to tell you something important.

Controlling your emotions is key. It is also helpful to try to reduce the number of surprises that could come your way. I've learned over the years of working with students that if you clarify some expectations in key areas before your student lands on campus, you'll be way ahead of the game. Ideally, you and your student would have begun these discussions when you started the college search in earnest. This allows sufficient time for everyone involved to get ready for a new way of thinking about how things are done as a family.

Here are some expectations to get clarity on with your student:

1. Which college to attend, and how the search will be conducted. Who is leading that effort? The person in your family who is leading the college search is typically the one who is most invested in the process and interested in a good outcome. Hopefully, that is your student. If you, the parent find yourself doing all or most of the research on colleges, calling the colleges to set up visits, and filling out your student's college applications—all of which I have seen quite a bit of in my career—you are doing your son or daughter a serious disservice. Cease and desist, immediately. You must put these responsibilities on your student if you expect him or her to own his or her college decision and take responsibility for it.

2. Selection of Major. Will your student have complete freedom to choose? Are you mandating, or perhaps heavily encouraging a certain major that you sense your son or daughter isn't really passionate about? If you are, I encourage you to ask yourself the question, Why am I trying to control this aspect of my student's life?

3. Money. Who pays for what? Tuition, books, room, board? What about spending money? Gas money for coming home or other family events that he or she is expected to attend? What about work—do you expect your student to get a part-time job?

4. Visits home. How often? What about family events? What is in-bounds and out-of-bounds during a visit home? Do you have the expectation that your son or daughter will spend every moment with you on breaks, or do you have a different expectation? How aware are you of your student's expectations about this?

PARENT DEBRIEF

As you go through the following debrief questions, please remember that some will be more relevant to your situation than others.

1 What did you resonate with in this chapter? Why?

2 What surprised you?

3 What new insights do you need to process further?

4 What actions would you consider taking as a result of these new insights?

5 What are some areas where you and your son or daughter need to get on the same page regarding: the college search, major selection, money, etc.?

6 How emotionally self-aware are you? That is, to what extent are you aware of cause and effect regarding your own emotions and what "triggers" set you off? Where can you improve in this area as you communicate with your college student?

FOUR

SEEK TO UNDERSTAND YOUR STUDENT'S GOD-GIVEN, UNIQUE WIRING

Lattes at the Davis Student Center Café the next week couldn't come quickly enough for Kyle. He had experienced what felt like a major breakthrough with his parents, and he couldn't wait to tell Katie about it in person. Of course he had already shared the gist of the story through a text conversation with her earlier in the week, but since they had agreed to try to replace text dialogues with real, live conversation—in person, or on the phone—now he had the opportunity to tell her more.

She was barely seated when Kyle jumped right in. "Katie! I felt like this day couldn't get here fast enough. I just can't believe how well things seem to be going between me and my parents."

Katie was almost as enthused as he was. "I know! This is such great news. Tell me more about how things went in that last phone call with your parents—the one you were texting me about."

"Yeah, and thanks for reminding me that we're trying to actually talk about the important stuff instead of texting it. Well, it went kind of like this: I knew something was different right from the start. Mom wasn't asking me all the usual 'hovering' kinds of questions I was used to when she calls. In fact, Dad was the first to talk this time. He asked if I was doing okay, and then shared that he and Mom had attended a conference specifically for parents of recently launched, and soon-to-launch, college students. He said your parents were there, too."

Katie was half-pleased and half-puzzled by this news. "Really? That's great . . . and weird at the same time. My parents didn't say anything about this to me."

"Well, the conference was this past Saturday," Kyle pointed out. "And today is Tuesday . . . don't you usually talk to them on Thursday evenings? I'm sure they'll tell you about it when you talk with them."

"I guess . . . it's still kind of weird they didn't tell me about it in our call *last* Thursday evening. I mean, they would have known they were going to attend at that point. You would think they would have mentioned it since it has to do with me," Katie explained in an irritated tone.

"Now wait a second, Katie," urged Kyle. "What about all that talk several weeks ago about developing independence and healthy boundaries with our parents? Doesn't that go both ways? I mean, doesn't it seem like a kind of double standard if you expect that your parents be okay with you not telling them *everything* that's going on in your life, but then you're offended when they don't tell you everything they're doing?"

Katie squirmed playfully and stuck her tongue out at her friend. She knew he had a point. "I'm not offended . . . just irritated. But I guess I shouldn't be."

"*Anyway*, back to me," Kyle teased. "My parents were telling me a good bit of what they had taken away from this launch-your-college-student thing."

"Ok, well, spill it—I'm all ears," Katie responded in a somewhat impatient tone.

"First, Dad apologized to me. It really took me off-guard. His apologies are pretty few and far between. He said he regretted not understanding the deep purposes of a college education—until now. Before the conference, he had been assuming what most people think of when they hear the word *college*—that it is basically what you have to know in order to get into a decent career. Dad said that, because of what he'd learned at the conference about how most of the colleges and universities in this country were established to educate us as whole persons—as image-bearers of God—he realized that he'd been selling me short on a compelling vision for what my college years could really be. Instead of casting an exciting vision for my education and how I would grow as a whole person, including my intellect, character, and sense of calling in the world, he had been seeing college *only* as a way to get a credential so that I could be okay financially after college. Well, all that is very different in his mind now. And guess who helped him get there? *Your father*."

"What? Really? Unbelievable! And it's so cool to see your father re-thinking all of it." Katie remarked.

"I know!" said Kyle. "I'm surprised, too. But I think Dad is even more surprised by his change of perspective than I am. Ever since I've known him he has been so driven, so into his work, and making things happen for his company. I've admired him for that, even though he wasn't around at home as much as I would've liked. Ever since we really started talking about my college plans during my junior year of high school, he has always been adamant that I needed to major in something that will actually 'get me hired.'

> Most of the colleges and universities in this country were established to educate us as whole persons—as image-bearers of God.

So him saying that he wants more for me during my college years than just a way to 'credentialize' myself for the job market comes as a real shocker to me."

"Yeah, that's a big shift. It sounds like he's not so concerned anymore about you getting a job after college," Katie said.

Kyle was quick to correct his friend's misunderstanding. "Oh no, I wouldn't go that far. That's not it at all. He's still concerned about that, and he's asking questions about how I'm planning to network, get internships, work experience, and all that. It's just that the conference and continuing conversations with your dad helped him to see that the best kind of college education is designed to help grow and flourish as human beings, not just become paycheck-making machines after the 'training' is over. So what he and I talk about now is mostly about how I'm growing as a person as a result of my classes, extracurriculars, and volunteering . . . in addition to how I'm thinking proactively about full-time work following graduation."

"That's amazing. Sounds to me like those conversations could even be fun."

"Most of the time, they are!" Kyle exclaimed. "The coolest part is that, for the first time, Dad is seeing how my growth as a whole person is connected to how God has 'wired' me. He's encouraging me to see college as a journey where I'm discovering my unique interests, strengths, and talents as I go through school in order to discern my calling."

"That is super-cool, Kyle. Sounds a lot like the kinds of things my parents have been talking with me about, too," Katie observed.

"Maybe, except your parents have been saying this kind of stuff to you for a while now. So you're used to thinking in these ways. Now, they're helping my parents to understand it better," Kyle replied.

"Yeah, okay, you have a point." Katie nodded in agreement, eyebrows raised. "But just because they've been sharing it doesn't mean I was always ready to receive it. What's that old saying I've heard some of my professors say over and over again? Something like 'when the student is ready, the teacher will appear.' I'm pretty sure that my parents wanted to teach me more during high school, but I just wasn't really in a student mindset. So, tell me more about what your Dad was saying to you about finding your strengths in college—that's interesting."

"What's really interesting to me," Kyle replied, "is that he's doing a whole lot less telling and a lot more question-asking than I've experienced from him in the past—like, ever. I mean, he's asking good questions about the ways I'm seeing myself grow during my time here, and what strengths I'm noticing that I could continue to grow and leverage for my future. That's pretty huge for both him and me."

"That's awesome, Kyle, but what do you mean by 'pretty huge'?"

"Well, for him, it means that he's trying to get into my world through asking good questions, rather than imposing his world on me. It's not that I don't want his ideas, but until now, his usual way of dispensing advice was to assume that I should do college exactly the same way he did. He's been assuming that since he has been so successful, I should just follow the exact same steps so that I'd turn out to be just as successful as him. I used to hear a lot of 'shoulds' from him, like 'you should be taking more business classes,' or 'you should try to get into student government right away,' and 'you shouldn't be wasting your time on meaningless things like intramural sports.' You can see why that was a problem for me," Kyle explained.

"Definitely," Katie said. "So back to my question, what's 'pretty huge' for you?"

"It means that his good questions are getting me to think for myself now. He has acknowledged that I'll be living out my own God-given calling, and that is probably going to look different from his. So now, instead of me being so worried about following his method of doing things exactly his way, his open-ended, open-handed questions have freed me to pursue my own methods based on the way I'm naturally wired. He even quoted a scripture passage to me on the phone: Proverbs 22:6, 'Train up a child in the way he should go, and when he is old he will not depart from it.'"

Katie was confused. "Wait, I've always thought that passage was mostly talking about how parents should raise their kids in a way that is good, right, and true according to the Bible and all that. How is that related to how you're 'naturally wired'?"

"Yeah, I used to think that same thing about that passage of the Bible," Kyle explained. "I thought that it was only talking about how kids won't stray from the truth if the parents are consistent in the way they teach, discipline, and encourage. But that's not the whole story—at the college launch conference our parents went to, one of the speakers pointed out something not many people realize about that verse. 'In the way he should go' implies a paved way—a way paved by the child's unique personality."[11]

Katie gave Kyle a look of half-disbelief, half-delight as she said, "No way. I have *always* thought that verse was just another way of the Bible commanding parents to raise their kids the right way, under God, and the church, and all that stuff. How could it be referring to a child's unique personality?"

Kyle explained further. "Dad told me that, according to the conference speaker, the verse in the original Hebrew has been studied a lot by biblical scholars, and that the verse is encouraging parents to help each child recognize his or her unique gifts, in light of God's principles, of course. When I thought about that for a while, the part that says 'when he is old he will not depart from it' made more sense than ever before. Our unique gifts are the tendencies, interests, and strengths that we naturally want to use, and if our parents encourage us to leverage those well as we grow up, it makes sense that we wouldn't 'depart' from those ways of living. In other words, as they encourage us to use the intellectual strengths, spiritual gifts, and unique wiring God has given *us*, it's like they are galvanizing us and making the raw materials inside of us blend together better so that we're even stronger."

As Kyle paused to take a breath, a silent Katie waited for him to continue. "And," Kyle added, "Dad drove the point home that the college launch conference speakers really emphasized: That college is a *key* time to be identifying and practicing the way we learn, work, and relate to others . . . and to God, in the way that He has uniquely designed us."

"That makes *so* much sense to me," Katie grinned. "Why didn't we hear about this in church? I've never heard a sermon on the value of identifying and using our unique wiring."

"I know, it stinks that we're only really hearing about this when we're already in college. But maybe we're hearing it sooner than most people. And, like you said before, it's a fair question to ask whether we students would've been ready for the 'teachers to appear' on this subject before now.

Finishing their lattes, the two friends parted ways. "See you next week, same time, same place," a cheery Kyle said.

"Sure thing!" Katie shouted back to him as she walked to her next class.

Implications for real life: The "Shoulds" Path vs. Your Student's Unique Strengths Path

Here, we saw Kyle experience a weight lifted off his shoulders. For the first time, he felt set free to explore his own unique set of gifts and strengths in college. Through a conference and continuing conversation with Jim, Kyle's father Tom was beginning to understand for the first time the deeper purposes of a college education and how those related to the way in which Kyle could use his college years to explore his unique wiring for the sake of finding God's call for his life.

As someone who has taught and coached college students since 2002, I've had too many conversations with students whose parents are pushing them with the "shoulds" that Kyle was talking about. "You should major in pre-med," or "you shouldn't major in psychology, since you can't get a good paying job with just a bachelor's degree in that." I've even heard "you should come home more often than you do; we see your friends from other colleges here at home all the time on the weekends." You know what the "shoulds" do for your student, Mom and Dad? In my experience, if that's the tone with which you're communicating to them most of the time, they tend to do one of two things. They either conform to parental wishes, or reject the *shoulds* and risk having you mad at them for not following the path they "should" have followed in college. When they conform to the *shoulds*, they tend to guard themselves emotionally instead of opening themselves up to you.

I've also seen the joy that students experience when parents understand the true meaning of "train up a child in the way he should go" and act accordingly. Everyone wins when this happens. Who are these parents, and what do they do differently from others? Although much more could be said, I believe it boils down to three main things.

First, these parents know that their children are a gift from God and that ultimately they belong to God. These fathers and mothers have a profound conviction that their children were theirs to steward for a season. But that is the key—it is only for a season. They do not continue to hold on in ways that prove to be impediments for their student's growth. Just as the Old Testament figure Hannah in 1 Samuel 1 returned her very young son to God after only a short season of raising him, so these parents know that their children will be with them for a short season—and then it will be time to turn them loose and allow them to carry out their God-given callings.

> When they conform to the shoulds, they tend to guard themselves emotionally instead of opening themselves up to you.

Second, these parents are secure in themselves and have a fairly high degree of self-awareness. They are the men and women who, with God's help, have wrestled their inner demons to the ground and are stronger as a result of the hardship. They learned long ago that they are not the center of the universe. There is no place for narcissism in their world, least of all in their offspring. They love their kids, but their kids are not their entire world. They understand where their kids end and they begin. That is to say, these parents work hard to make sure that healthy boundaries are in place. This is absolutely critical. I have observed so much pain and dysfunction in college students because of parents who just refused to "get" this.

Finally, these are the parents who maintain a natural curiosity about their children. Rather than trying to fit each of their kids into any preconceived categories or roles, these parents allow their curiosity to take them places that more controlling parents are often uncomfortable with. They know that they will negatively impact their student's college experience by trying to shelter them, controlling their destiny, or vicariously living the life through their student they wished they had chosen. Being curious about how God has designed their son or daughter helps them remember that college is about their student discerning God's call and becoming a person of virtue and wisdom who will seek to serve others.

PARENT DEBRIEF

As you go through the following debrief questions, please remember that some will be more relevant to your situation than others.

1 What was your main take-away from this chapter?

2 What are the ways in which you have encouraged your current or soon-to-be college student to explore, identify, and leverage his or her God-given, unique blend of personality characteristics and strengths?

3 Get honest here: Where have you possibly (even unintentionally) punished or discouraged your college student for not doing something the way they "should" have done it? How often do you tell your son or daughter what major he or she "should" choose, or which career he or she "should" pursue? How could you get rid of the "shoulds"?

FIVE

ENCOURAGE MENTORING RELATIONSHIPS OUTSIDE OF YOUR FAMILY

The following week came and went quickly, and the two friends once again found themselves ordering their favorite lattes at the campus café.

"How was your week, Kyle?" asked Katie.

Kyle smiled as he answered. "Can't complain, it was pretty okay, all-in-all. How about yours?"

"Kind of mixed, actually—okay academically, but fantastic on a relationship-building level."

Kyle was intrigued. "Well, are you going to keep me in suspense?"

"You pay better attention if I do," Katie joked, with a smirk. "Okay, here it is. Let me get the 'okay' part out of the way first, then we'll talk about the fun stuff."

"Fair enough," Kyle said.

"I got a *C* on my mid-term calculus exam, and *B*-minus on my biology exam," Katie said sheepishly, her bottom lip poked out purposefully so as to evoke Kyle's sympathy.

"Ugh. Sorry about that, Katie," he said softly. "I know you had been studying hard for both of those."

Katie nodded in agreement. "Yeah, well, I've about decided that I'm just *not* a math and science person. I'm doing great in all my humanities courses; maybe I'm just more of a reader-writer type than a numbers-analytical type."

"That may be," Kyle acknowledged in a slightly frustrated tone. "But, don't you think it's a little early in your college career to make that call? I mean, seriously, we've only been here for ten weeks. Plus, you don't need to be letting yourself off the hook like that."

Katie, with a frown on her face, pushed back. "Okay, fine, I see your point. But I can say with confidence that I'm not really enjoying those courses right now."

"I get it," Kyle said. "I don't like my English lit class, and right now I'm only pulling a *B*-minus in there. So we're in the same boat. Let's get to the 'fun stuff' about your week?"

"Woo-hoo!" Katie shouted, throwing her hands up in the air in raising-the-roof style. "I got a mentor!"

"A mentor?" Kyle responded, somewhat deflated. "Um, that's . . . great." Kyle was trying to sound excited for his friend, but he couldn't hide the confusion on his face.

Katie, with a playfully disappointed face, leaned in Kyle's direction. "Can't you be more excited than that, Kyle? C'mon, this is a big deal for me!"

"Ok, I'm sorry! I *am* glad for you, but I don't totally get it. I know what a mentor is, or at least I think I do, but I'm not sure why that would be so exciting."

Katie almost didn't let Kyle finish his sentence. "I'll tell you why it's so exciting. I get to learn from an older and wiser person for my entire college career. Joanna is someone who's lived in town here for fifteen years or so, and she's a wife, mother, and she works part-time, too. Before she had kids, she was vice-president of a bank. I met her at church a few Sundays ago and we really hit it off. We're going to meet together for lunch every other week. I can't wait for our first one!"

"So, you said you met at church, but how did the subject of mentoring come up? Did she just come up to you and say 'You look like you need a mentor?' And why do think you need a mentor, anyway?"

Now Kyle was genuinely excited for his friend, but he had a puzzled look on his face. Katie pressed him on what his expression meant. "Well," Kyle replied, "I see how proactive you're being with Joanna, pursuing her as a mentor, and that's great. I guess I'm just not seeing that kind of initiative as it comes to pursuing your professors as academic mentors, especially in the subjects where you're having some trouble right now. Can Joanna help you with your academics?"

"That's not the kind of mentor she is going to be for me. That's not what I want from her," Katie snapped, now irritated. "And no, she didn't just come up to me at church and see me as her 'project.' I had been looking for a mentor to help me think through some things as I transition from living at home to making college my interim home."

Kyle ignored his friend's frustration with his failure to catch on quickly. He was genuinely curious about this mentoring idea. He asked, "So, basically, Joanna is going to be like your life coach now, right?"

> A mentor is usually an older person who takes a younger person under his or her wing and gives to that younger person some of what God has given that mentor—whether it's wisdom, counsel, or a specific skill of some kind.

Katie's face softened a bit. "That's a good question," she replied. "It's not quite the same. During the life coaching my parents and I did together, our coach explained that coaching was all about helping others to unlock their potential in order to move forward in a certain area of life. Or even several areas. That is usually accomplished through the coach asking a *lot* of really good questions and helping the client find the way that's right for him or her. A mentor is usually an older person who takes a younger person under his or her wing and gives to that younger person some of what God has given that mentor—whether it's wisdom, counsel, or a specific skill of some kind. My coach said that many people find that it is helpful to have both a coach and a mentor, or even several mentors, depending on what the younger person wants from the mentoring relationship."

"Ok, so let me get this straight," Kyle responded, more interested. "Coaching isn't the same as mentoring, and you can have different mentors for different purposes?"

"You got it," Katie said affirmingly. "I'm starting off with just one mentor—Joanna. But I've got a couple of friends here who have two or three mentors. Sometimes, you want to have a mentor for spiritual things, then, say another mentor for academics, and maybe one for a hobby you're trying to learn. The main point is to have someone older and wiser in your life from whom you can learn."

"Okay, I get it, kind of," Kyle said, half-confidently. "In the way you've just described it, why wouldn't you just have one of your parents be your mentor? Assuming you get along with them well, of course. Am I not getting it? Is that a dumb question?"

"No, it isn't a dumb question, Kyle. Most people our age really aren't familiar with the concept of mentoring at all. Sure, they have parents and bosses from work and teachers and other older adults in their lives. But, for the most part, they have not seen those relationships as opportunities to lean into. To answer your question about parents being mentors—it's not that they *can't* be mentors; however, they just shouldn't be the only ones you have. Think about it this way: Even though they're not perfect by any means, you and I both have good parents. They have taught us a lot, and they can continue to teach us some important things. But they are not all-knowing. Even though they know us well, they can't see everything in us that we could be in the future. They don't know how to do everything that you and I are gifted to do."

Kyle was leaning back and smiling at this point. "Okay, I get it now, for real. You're so right, Katie. I know I need my parents for some things, but I'm

> It is rare for a college freshman to walk onto campus with a proactive mindset.

seeing how I need other men who are further along than me in certain areas to help me along the way. There are things that I'd like to learn from some older and wiser guy than me, and I know I can't really learn those things from my Dad."

Katie nodded. "You got it, all right. Is there some older guy you know right now who you could see yourself connecting with and learning from on a regular basis?"

"I need to think a little more about it, but yeah, I think so," Kyle replied.

Implications for Real Life

It is rare for a college freshman to walk onto campus with a proactive mindset. Most are not intentional about their academics, but they know they have to do the work in order to stay in school. If a student doesn't "have" to pursue something in college, then it is likely that he or she won't. I have found that students have to be nudged a bit to pursue mentoring relationships. As we saw in the dialogue between Katie and Kyle, Kyle just wasn't at all familiar with the concept of mentoring, at least as something that he ought to consider pursuing of his own initiative. He needed his friend to introduce him to the idea, and then he got curious. That's how it happens much of the time—word-of-mouth.

I have taught and coached students whose parents introduced them to the concept and practice of mentoring way before they left home for college. These students are the ones who generally hit the ground running. If they have had a good experience with mentors in middle school and/or high school, they will come to college looking for mentors.

There is great potential in a mentoring relationship where there is maximum alignment between a student and mentor in three areas: character (values alignment),

> You have the power to encourage healthy mentoring relationships.

chemistry (personality alignment), and competence (alignment of interests). I have personally served as a mentor, and I have been mentored as well. I have taught and coached students who sought a mentor or multiple mentors and capitalized on those relationships for all they were worth. Those are the students who flourish the most—the ones who "get after it" with enthusiasm.

Whatever the case may be for your now-adult child, and whatever his or her familiarity may be with mentoring, your influence matters. You have the power to encourage healthy mentoring relationships. You also have the power to discourage your student—whether through criticism, possessiveness, or apathy—from branching out and learning from others. Which will you choose?

PARENT DEBRIEF

As you go through the following debrief questions, please remember that some will be more relevant to your situation than others.

1 How are you encouraging your college student to pursue mentoring relationships outside of your family?

2 On a scale of one to ten, please rate yourself honestly on how possessive you feel of your son or daughter. From one (not possessive at all) to ten (extremely possessive). In what ways could you be unintentionally sabotaging your student's efforts to get to know older mentors outside of your family unit?

3 What kind of mentor is your student most likely to pursue?

4 What kinds of mentors does your student still need? Spiritual? Academic? Work?

SIX

TAKE THE LONG VIEW

I t was now early December, six weeks or so after their first back-yard barbeque. Tom and Cindy invited Jim and Sandra over for another evening of steaks, relaxation, and catching up. A lot had happened since their early fall get-together, including the college launch conference (that Katie and Kyle talked about in chapter four), and everyone was eager for the reunion.

The four friends exchanged pleasantries at first, and then the two men excused themselves to tend to the steaks while the ladies finished up in the kitchen. Jim and Tom quickly settled on the back porch; predictably, Tom was the first to get the conversation rolling. He flipped the steaks as he launched in.

"So, how's it going, Jim? It's been too long since we've really talked. Of course we saw each other at the conference, but we didn't really get to catch up."

"It's pretty good I'd say, Tom," Jim replied. "At least, overall it's good."

"That's great, but I sense a bit of hesitancy in the way you said that. What's up?"

To Jim's surprise, and in uncharacteristic fashion, Tom followed up with a probing question. In the ten years they had been friends, Jim had never really known Tom to be a very good question-asker, so Jim was caught a bit off-guard.

"Oh, it's really nothing," Jim assured him. "I guess Sandra and I have just been missing our Katie a good bit lately."

Tom again surprised Jim again, this time by empathizing. "Yeah, I know what you mean. Cindy and I have been feeling the same about Kyle being gone. It's just hard, isn't it?"

"Sure is," Jim quickly agreed. "I've never known Sandra to cry very much, but she's done more crying in the last several months since our last backyard get-together than I think she's done in all our years being married."

"I totally get it!" Tom chuckled in agreement. "For Cindy and me, it looks a bit different, but we still aren't used to Kyle not being here. It took us six weeks worth of grocery trips before we finally remembered to stop buying four gallons of milk on each visit to the store. And there were even at least two times that Cindy was at the check-out counter and realized she had five or six of his regular go-to snacks, and she had to go put them back!"

"Oh, that's classic!" Jim said as he chuckled along with his friend. "We haven't exactly experienced that challenge, but we have caught ourselves a few times waiting in the car for Katie when we're ready to go somewhere, then we remember she's at college. She was always running late and so when we were going somewhere together, it was common for us to sit in the driveway waiting on her, with the car idling."

"That's hilarious," Tom said. His tone shifted from playful to somewhat serious. "You know, Jim, I've been doing a lot of thinking lately."

"Oh?"

"Yes, quite a bit of thinking," Tom continued. And, I have to credit you with starting me down this road. Remember our last get-together here?"

"Sure! How couldn't I remember it?" Jim responded energetically, "We had such a great discussion; at least you and I did. I think our wives excused themselves from our conversation right after dessert was over though."

Tom nodded. "Yep. That was the talk that got me started down this road. After you and Sandra left that evening, I kept thinking about our conversation. I didn't fully understand everything you had said about the deep purpose of a college education and all that, but this question kept haunting me."

"What question?"

"The question that keeps going through my head is, *What if I've been shallow regarding the meaning of education, work, and how God is involved in all of it?*" Tom replied.

Jim was intrigued. "Okay, I don't see you as a shallow person, but please go on. I think I need to hear more."

"Well," Tom continued enthusiastically, "I've been thinking that for so many years I've been working, working, working, and never stopping. I just love to work!"

"I get that, Tom," Jim said patiently. "But I'm still not connecting the dots."

Tom slowed down, lowering his voice. "What I'm trying to say is that for as long as I can remember in my working life, all I've ever known is how to build a business, make it grow, achieve, and make it better and better, all the while never giving any thought to slowing down. Because I've always been going so fast in my achiever mode, I've never really slowed down to think about, well, deeper things that require a break from go, go, go all the time."

"All right, now I'm beginning to see where you're headed," Jim assured him.

As the steaks were finishing, Cindy and Sandra emerged from the kitchen with the side dishes, and the four friends took

their places at the table as Tom kept his verbal stream of conscious-
ness going.

"For example," he continued, "for decades, it has never occurred
to me that college was anything more than a fancy training center
for future laborers in various occupations. Now, I see that view is
pretty shallow. If we are made in God's image, and if what it means
to live as image-bearers includes doing meaningful work to His glory, then how could education *not* take into account subjects that
help us understand more about our own humanity—subjects like
what you've studied, Jim?"

Sandra interrupted, "Tom, you mean Jim's double major in
Bible and philosophy?"

"Yes, exactly," Tom replied.

"Wow, Tom, you're really blowing me away here," Jim said
with a tone of delightful surprise. "You're speaking a different lan-
guage compared to what we heard you say about education a couple
months ago."

Cindy spoke up. "Yes, I'm surprised, too. But Tom, how do we
help Kyle understand all this now? What does he think he's sup-
posed to be doing at college?"

"Funny you should bring that up," he replied to Cindy. "I hav-
en't had a chance to tell you, but he and I had a great phone call not
long ago where we talked openly about all this. I shared with him
our main takeaways from the college launch conference we attended together and then apologized to him for all the pushing I've done
to get him to go in the direction I thought best instead of encouraging him to follow God's call."

"You had *that kind of conversation* with Kyle?" Cindy asked in
near disbelief.

"Sure did," Tom said proudly with a grin. "And, I was actually a
good listener!"

Sandra said, "Tom, I just have to say, well done. I'm sure that conversation sent a great message to Kyle."

"Absolutely," Jim quickly agreed.

"I sure hope so," Tom said. "My concern right now is how to keep preaching this message to myself so that I don't get too nervous about Kyle's future. As much as I love this new way of understanding what good education is, I'm still a bit anxious about how he will support himself."

"I get it," Jim empathized. "This concern surfaced with Sandra and I as Katie was going through her college search. The life coach we hired to help us through the search process led us through a powerful process of question-asking that helped us to see how we needed to handle that anxiety."

Cindy leaned in and asked, "So, how do you handle it?"

Sandra confidently yet calmly replied, "We've had to learn to take the long view of Katie's future."

"Long view, huh? Can you say more about that?" Tom inquired.

"Well," Sandra continued, "we—myself in particular—were feeling pretty stressed out during Katie's college search process. The coach we hired asked great questions that helped me to see that a lot of the anxiety was coming from fear."

"Fear of what, Sandra?" Cindy asked.

Sandra's eyes welled up with tears, but she didn't lose her composure. "Fear that Katie might not be okay once she is on her own."

"Okay, I get it. I totally understand that," Cindy said.

Jim held Sandra's hand as she continued, "So the way that looked, my fears were making Katie even more of a nervous wreck during the college application process. Thankfully, our life coach helped me identify the pattern."

"Pattern?" Tom said with a tone of curiosity.

Sandra explained, "Yes, for years and years, I've had a pattern of blowing up and running roughshod over Katie when I'm engaging her from a place of fear—something I'm afraid of—for example, my fear that she won't okay living on her own at college. When I'm motivated by fear, inevitably I resort to using facts and force

> Finding what you're passionate about and letting that be your main motivator will be far more lasting than fear, facts, and force.

to strong arm her into my way of seeing and doing things. This happened several times in the college search process, but with our life coach's help I got it under control. But, I am ashamed to say I'm struggling with it again now that Katie is gone. In fact, I blew up with her on the phone not long ago, and right before she was about to go to class."

"So, fear, facts, and force, huh?" Tom quietly replied. "That's the pattern?"

"Yep, pretty much," Sandra said, smiling. "I'm still a work in progress."

Tom quickly said, "Well, you've pricked my conscience, because I can definitely see how I lapse into that pattern myself when I get nervous about Kyle's future."

Jim jumped into the conversation. "Our coach helped us to see that while fear, facts, and force is one way of motivating people, it almost always results superficial and temporary change."

Tom was about to ask a follow-up question when Sandra jumped in ahead of him. "I know what you're about to ask, Tom—'what's a long-lasting motivation for change and growth?' So glad you asked!" she teased, then her expression became serious again. "It's *passion*. Finding what you're passionate about and letting that be your main motivator will be far more lasting than fear, facts, and force."

Cindy said, "I love it. That really resonates with me."

"I agree," Tom chimed in "It wouldn't have resonated with me so much a few months ago, but I totally see it now."

"But there's a catch to this passion thing," Sandra warned.

"What's that?" Tom asked.

"Like we were saying a few minutes ago—you have to take the long view of the future. Discovering and capitalizing on deeply held, God-given passion can be a long process, kind of like making a good stew," Sandra explained.

Everyone kept listening. She continued, "For example, my mother made the best beef stew I've ever tasted. It wasn't just the ingredients that made it good—it was the slow process of simmering of all those ingredients together that unlocked their unique flavors to make the stew what it was. One time, she was in a hurry and tried to speed up the process by turning up the heat. It just didn't taste good."

Tom spoke up. "So, this makes sense to me. We can't just turn up the heat on Katie and Kyle and expect that they will find what they are really passionate about any faster."

"Right," Jim said. "It's a process. If we turn the heat up too much, we may get compliance from them, but not authenticity or passion. And while some students are clear about their passions and God's call going into college, most really aren't. You'll remember at the college launch conference we attended, one of the coaches pointed out that most college students choose a major based one of two things: a) what is most expedient and easy, or b) what they think will make others happy. Since so many young people in this millennial generation are conflict-avoiders, they don't want to speak up about their interests and passions if they think it is going to disappoint someone in their family—mostly, their parents."

Tom replied, "Then it sounds like we have to be in this process with the long view in mind, just like you're saying."

Sandra said, "That's right. And, we have to keep the long view in mind about other things in Katie's and Kyle's lives as well, such as whether they are proactively seeking mentors, whether they're making good choices with their time, and so on."

Cindy spoke up. "I can see how taking the long view could be helpful to me and Tom as we're getting used to Kyle being away— specifically regarding ways *we* need to change as parents."

Tom perked up, "Such as?"

"Well, throughout this conversation, I've been thinking about how my people-pleasing tendencies and desire to keep the peace at all costs is really a short-term view. For too long, I've done whatever I think is going to maintain peace in the moment, without really looking at the life patterns I might be setting in our family." Cindy began to get teary, but Tom could tell she still wanted to engage.

"Go on, dear, it's okay," Tom reassured.

"Well, Tom," Cindy said, "This may be hard for you to hear, but it's even harder for me to say. I've not been taking a long view of our family as it comes to Kyle's brother. Every time Brian gets into a jam, I lean on Kyle to help me because I sense you don't want to deal with it. Kyle is always compliant and agrees to help me. For the last couple of years, I've sensed that you're okay with this dynamic, since you're always so busy with work. I've made the choice to keep the peace between the two of us on this issue, but based on that phone call we had with him a few weeks ago, now I'm afraid it has really taken a toll on him. Kyle doesn't feel like he can say *no*. At least that's what we both came away with from that conversation, right? You and I still haven't talked about it since that call."

"I know, and I blame myself for that, Cindy." Tom said apologetically. "We need to work through this together more intentionally. And I need to be more proactive as a husband and father on this issue. You've been too dependent on Kyle regarding Brian's problems because I've been pretty passive in this area of our family."

"Good! Cindy exclaimed. "And I need help from all of you in learning how to be more assertive and speaking up more. Kyle told me recently in a phone call that he sees how he 'plays the victim' when he can't have his way sometimes, and in certain cases he uses it to avoid healthy conflict. He was wondering why I do the same thing. I'm sure he gets it from me! I don't want to be this way anymore."

There was a longer than usual pause in the conversation. Jim finally broke the silence.

"Well, I had no idea when we began our evening together what we'd talk about, but this has been pretty rich," Jim began. "Certainly none of us are perfect parents, but it's clear that we do love our now-adult kids and want the best for them. One thing this evening has done for me is given me a greater sense of hope for Katie's and Kyle's future. I for one, think we have a lot to celebrate."

"I totally agree, Jim," Tom said. "Why don't we plan to do this together on a quarterly basis? I've learned a ton this evening, and I'd like to continue that. After all, that would be in the spirit of maintaining the long view, right?"

Everyone was excited about this idea. Cindy said "Tom and Jim, do the two of you want to look at possible dates for our next dinner while Sandra and I get dessert and coffee?" The four friends continued their evening of fellowship together, and resolved to make their dinners together a regular priority.

Conclusion: Implications for Real Life

How often do we take the long view in life? It isn't easy, especially when things are aren't going so well. Very often, our temptation is to trade in the long-term good for a short-term win. As we saw with the final dialogue of this book, each parent was seeing how their patterns of slipping into short-term thinking was producing less than ideal results in their relationships. We also saw how, as the conversation unfolded, each person became increasingly trusting of the others and felt safe enough to speak openly about issues that matter. Going to college isn't just about your student; it is also about *you* as a parent, because it means, among other things, that you've succeeded in helping your son or daughter get to this point. That's something to celebrate. It's also about you in that you will continue to have a relationship with your son or daughter. You have the opportunity now to continue healthy patterns and break unhealthy ones.

> Everyone's college launch story has coauthors.

Everyone's college launch story has coauthors. With God's help, you, as a parent (or parents) are coauthoring the story with your student. Each of you will contribute to the story in some way or other. Whatever becomes a part of your unique story is a function of what you create or what you allow, for better or worse. It is about how you choose to adjust to the change, because that will affect your student one way or another.

Take some time to work through debrief on the following page.

PARENT DEBRIEF

What are your main takeaways from this last chapter?

1 How much of a factor has fear been in the college launch process? Fear on whose part, specifically? What does that fear look like, and what effects has it had on your family?

2 What are a few new insights you've had about your student's college launch story as you have read through this book? Where would you say things are going well? Where have you seen success? How could you capitalize further on those successes?

3 What hasn't gone so well thus far in the college launch? Remember to ask the question "In this situation, what am I creating, and what am I allowing?" Consider brainstorming some ideas for how you could improve the situation. Then review your ideas with someone who you trust will give you honest feedback on them.

4 Where do you experience stress related to your student's college transition?

5 Where do you experience joy and hope related to your student's college transition?

6 How are you celebrating this new season?

ENDNOTES

1   Genesis 1:28. This verse stands as the basis for what the Christian tradition has called the cultural mandate.

2   See Gary Gutting, *Why College is Not a Commodity. The Chronicle of Higher Education; The Chronicle Review.* September 11, 2015.

3   Gene C. Fant, Jr., *The Liberal Arts: A Student's Guide* (Wheaton: Crossway, 2012), p. 96.

4   Andy Crouch, *Culture Making: Recovering Our Creative Calling* (Downers Grove: IVP Press, 2013), pp. 257–258.

5   Korrell Kanoy, Steven J. Stein, & Howard E. Book, *The Student EQ Edge:Emotional Intelligence & Your Academic & Personal Success. Facilitation and Activity Guide.* San Francisco: Jossey-Bass, 2013) Kindle.

6   Sarah Eisner, "What's Worse Than Helicopter Parenting? Drone Parenting: When Becoming a More Present Parent Makes You a Worse One." *Fast Company*, October 14, 2015. http://www.fastcompany.com/3051609/second-shift/whats-worse-than-helicopter-parenting-drone-parenting (accessed November 3, 2015)

7   Alan Mozes, "College students admit texting in the most inappropriate places," *HealthDay*. April 15, 2015. http://www. cbsnews.com/news/college-students-admit-texting-in-the-most-inappropriate-places/ (accessed November 3, 2015)

8   Patricia Somers and Jim Settle, "The Helicopter Parent (Part 2): International Arrivals and Departures," *College and University 86*, no. 2 (2010): pp. 2–9. http://eric. ed.gov/?id=EJ912004. Quoted in Julie Lythcott-Haims, *How To Raise An Adult: Break Free of the Overparenting Trap and Prepare Your Kid for Success.* (New York: Henry Holt & Co., 2015). (accessed November 3, 2015)

9   Peter Gray, "Declining Student Resilience: A Serious Problem for Colleges," *Psychology Today*, September 22, 2015, https:// www.psychologytoday.com/blog/freedom-learn/201509/ declining-student-resilience-serious-problem-colleges (accessed October 27, 2015)

10 Tim Elmore, *Artificial Maturity: Helping Kids Meet the Challenge of Becoming Authentic Adults.* (San Francisco: Jossey-Bass, 2012), p. 44.

11 Garry K. Brantley, r 27, 2015)/blog/freedom-learn/201509/d, "*Apologetics Press*, 1995, https://www.apologeticspress.org/ apcontent.aspx?category=7&article=348 (accessed October 27, 2015)

About John D. Basie, Ph.D.

John D. Basie (Ph.D., Baylor University) is Director of the Scholars and Masters Programs at the Impact 360 Institute, an innovative organization that exists to impact culture by creating Christ-centered worldview and leadership opportunities. Impact 360 Institute is affiliated with Lifeshape, Inc., and Union University. He is also founder and principal of Millennial 360, LLC, a career and leadership-coaching firm for college students, graduate students, and young professionals. John has been formally working with college and graduate students since 2000, having served as a student life director, dean of enrollment, professor, and professional leadership and career coach. He is happily married to his college sweetheart, Marana. Together, with their three children and three dogs, they make their home in Pine Mountain, Georgia.

Twitter: @JohnBasie